W9-AGH-742

perfect wedding favors

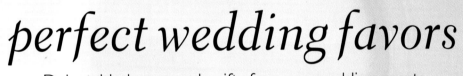

perfect wedding favors

Delectable homemade gifts for your wedding guests

Susannah Blake

photography by Carolyn Barber

LONDON · NEW YORK

Senior Designer Sonya Nathoo
Editor Rebecca Woods
Production Laura Grundy
Art Director Leslie Harrington
Editorial Director Julia Charles

Prop Stylist Liz Belton
Food Stylists Bridget Sargeson
and Jack Sargeson
Indexer Hilary Bird

First published in 2012 by
Ryland Peters & Small
519 Broadway, 5th Floor
New York, NY 10012

Text © Susannah Blake 2012
Design and photographs © Ryland
Peters & Small 2012

Printed in China

10 9 8 7 6 5 4 3 2 1

The author's moral rights have been
asserted. All rights reserved. No part of this
publication may be reproduced, stored in a
retrieval system or transmitted in any form
or by any means, electronic, mechanical,
photocopying, or otherwise, without the
prior permission of the publisher.

ISBN: 978-1-84975-286-2

US Library of Congress Cataloging-in-
publication data has been applied for

Notes
• All spoon measurements are level, unless
otherwise specified.
• Eggs are medium, unless otherwise
specified. Uncooked or partially cooked
eggs should not be served to the very old,
frail, young children, pregnant women, or
those with compromised immune systems.
• When a recipe calls for the grated zest
of citrus fruit, buy unwaxed fruit and wash
well before using. If you can find only
treated fruit, scrub well in warm soapy
water before using.
• To sterilize preserving jars and bottles,
wash them in hot, soapy water and rinse
in boiling water. Place in a large saucepan
and cover with hot water. With the pan lid
on, bring the water to a boil and continue
to boil for 15 minutes. Turn off the heat and
leave the jars or bottles in the hot water
until just before they are to be filled. Invert
the jars or bottles on a clean dish towel
to dry. Sterilize the lids for 5 minutes by
boiling, or according to the manufacturer's
instructions. Jars and bottles should be
filled and sealed while they are still hot.

contents

introduction

The tradition of a small gift from the bride and groom to wedding guests dates back centuries to the European aristocracy, when small, elaborate boxes containing sugar cubes or confections were given to guests. As time passed and sugar became a less valuable commodity, the tradition became more widespread and sugared almonds became the favor of choice for centuries. A classic wedding favor, even at modern weddings, is still five sugared almonds tied up in beautiful fabric, with each of the five almonds representing health, wealth, happiness, fertility, and longevity.

Today, wedding favors have become an intrinsic part of a wedding reception and can range from the simplest almonds or individual chocolate in a pretty gift box to more elaborate gifts personalized with the couple's names and wedding date. Whatever you choose though, presentation is always of the utmost importance, tying in with the theme of your wedding and the personalities of the bride and groom.

Even with all the planning in the world, the run-up to a wedding day can be fraught with last-minute panics and stresses. To avoid adding to those potential worries, make sure you're on top of the favor situation well ahead of time. Most of the recipes in this book need to be made just a few days before the wedding to ensure they are enjoyed at their very best. But you can avoid any nasty last-minute surprises by picking your chosen favor well ahead. At least a month before the wedding, have a trial run at making the recipe. Does it look and taste just as you want it to? Can you imagine making several batches without wanting to tear your hair out or sit down and weep in a corner? Give yourself plenty of time to find and order the perfect packaging. And if you're making the packaging from scratch, such as popcorn cones or little cellophane bags, I would recommend you make those well in advance.

With a little bit of planning, you can ensure that you have no nasty surprises when it comes to making your wedding favors, and you can simply enjoy relaxing and packaging up your favors the day before with family and friends.

*candies &
confectionery*

turkish delight

Glistening cubes of pale pink Turkish delight, delicately scented with rosewater, make a delightfully romantic wedding favor. To serve at the table, place each piece of Turkish delight on a fresh rose petal arranged on a serving dish. Alternatively, a few cubes placed in a gift box tied up with ribbon, perhaps with a few dried rose petals, looks equally pretty.

Put 1⅔ cups water in a large saucepan set over a low heat and add the rosewater and a little food coloring to make a vibrant pink. Sprinkle over the gelatin and sugar and heat gently, stirring occasionally, until the sugar has dissolved. Bring to a boil, then reduce the heat and simmer gently for 20 minutes.

When the mixture is ready, remove the pan from the heat and leave to cool for a couple of minutes. Skim off any foam from the top of the mixture then pour it into the prepared pan. Cover with plastic wrap and leave to set for 3 hours in the fridge.

When set, turn the Turkish delight out onto a chopping board and use a sharp knife to slice the square into 8 strips, then slice into 8 strips in the opposite direction to make 64 cubes. Combine the confectioners' sugar and cornstarch then sift onto a large plate. Toss each cube of Turkish delight in the confectioners' sugar mixture to coat.

Store the Turkish delight in an airtight container, layered between sheets of baking paper, until required. These can be made up to a week in advance.

2 tablespoons rosewater

pink food coloring

4 tablespoons powdered gelatin

3½ cups sugar

2 tablespoons confectioners' sugar

1 tablespoon cornstarch

an 8-inch square cake pan, greased

makes 64

violet and rose chocolate shards

6½ oz. semisweet
chocolate, broken
into chunks

crystallized rose and
violet petals, to decorate

*a baking sheet, lined with
non-stick baking paper*

makes about 50

These simple, spiky chocolate pieces, studded with sugary crystallized violet and rose petals, look so pretty arranged in a shallow dish or bowl. Create your own chocolate sculpture on the table by piling them up high in interesting shapes. Don't forget that chocolate melts very easily, so if you are having a summer wedding during blazingly hot weather, be sure to keep your chocolate shards cool.

Put the chocolate in a heatproof bowl set over a pan of barely simmering water. Leave the chocolate to stand until partially melted, then remove from the heat and stir until fully melted.

Pour the melted chocolate into the centre of the prepared baking sheet and gently spread out to about ⅛ inch thick. Sprinkle crystalized violet petals over half of the chocolate and crystallized rose petals over the other half, spacing them well apart.

Leave the chocolate to set at cool room temperature. When set but not hard, remove the chocolate slab from the baking sheet and use a sharp knife to slice it into long, delicate shards. You will end up with rose shards, violet shards, and probably some plain or mixed shards.

When the chocolate is completely hard, gently peel off the baking paper and store in an airtight container in the fridge until required. These can be made up to a week in advance.

vanilla-blueberry fudge

2½ cups sugar

¾ cup plus 1 tablespoon heavy cream

4 tablespoons butter

1 teaspoon vanilla extract

¾ cup dried blueberries

an 8-inch square cake pan, greased

makes 64

Fudge is a wonderfully simple pleasure that everyone loves. There's something a little bit childish and nostalgic about it—so why not look out for small jars in which to pile your fudge, such as old-fashioned candy jars, then top them with pretty fabric and a sprig of leaves or flowers.

Put the sugar, cream, and butter in a large saucepan and heat very gently, stirring occasionally until the butter has melted and the sugar dissolved. Bring the mixture to a boil, without stirring, and continue to heat gently until the mixture reaches 244°F. (If you don't have a sugar thermometer, drop a little of the syrup into a glass of chilled water. It should keep it's shape and form a soft, flexible ball.)

When the syrup is ready, take the saucepan off the heat and stir in the vanilla extract. Beat the mixture until it thickens, then stir in the blueberries. Tip the mixture into the prepared cake pan and spread it evenly, smoothing down with a palette knife. Leave to cool completely.

When cooled and set, turn the fudge out onto a chopping board and use a sharp knife to slice the square into 8 strips, then slice into 8 strips in the opposite direction to make 64 cubes. Store in an airtight container until required. These can be made up to a week in advance.

coconut ice candy

a 14-oz. can sweetened condensed milk

3½ cups unsweetened desiccated coconut

3 cups confectioners' sugar, sifted

pink food coloring

an 8-inch square cake pan, greased

makes 64

There's something wonderfully nostalgic about coconut ice candy and it can bring a deliciously kitsch and slightly cheeky feel to a wedding breakfast. Traditionally, coconut ice is pink and white striped and will look gorgeous piled up on little glass cake stands decorated with ribbon.

Put the condensed milk, coconut, and confectioners' sugar in a large mixing bowl and stir well to combine. It will make a very stiff mixture so will require a bit of work.

Spoon half of the mixture into the prepared cake pan and spread out in an even layer, pressing down well with the back of a spoon.

Add a few drops of pink food coloring to the remaining mixture and stir well to combine, adding more food coloring if necessary to achieve the desired shade. Spoon the pink mixture on top of the white and spread out evenly, pressing down well with the back of a spoon. Cover with plastic wrap and leave to set overnight.

Turn the coconut ice candy out onto a chopping board and use a sharp knife to slice the square into 8 strips, then slice into 8 strips in the opposite direction to make 64 cubes. Store in an airtight container until required. These can be made up to a week in advance.

sponge candy shards

6 tablespoons unsalted butter
⅓ cup golden or light corn syrup
¾ cup sugar
2 teaspoons baking soda

a baking sheet, greased with flavorless oil

makes about 40

Melt-in-the-mouth sponge candy is delicious served plain or drizzled with dark chocolate. Present shards in pretty gift boxes that match the color scheme of the wedding, or, for a simple, old-fashioned feel, you could package it in brown paper bags lined with pastel-colored tissue paper.

Put the butter, syrup, and sugar in a large saucepan and heat gently until melted and the sugar has dissolved. Bring to a boil for about 6 minutes, without stirring. Swirl the pan occasionally to achieve an even color, until the mixture is golden brown.

Remove the pan from the heat, quickly stir in the baking soda—being very careful as the mixture will bubble and expand rapidly—and immediately pour onto the prepared baking sheet. Leave to cool and set completely, then break into shards.

Store the sponge candy in an airtight container until required. These can be made up to a week in advance.

fresh strawberry marshmallows

1 cup strawberries, hulled

1 teaspoon lemon juice

2½ tablespoons powdered gelatin

2¼ cups sugar

⅔ cup golden or light corn syrup

4–5 tablespoons cornstarch, for dusting

a 10 x 9-inch baking pan, lined with plastic wrap and greased

a sheet of plastic wrap large enough to cover the baking pan, greased

a smaller, round cookie cutter (optional)

makes about 130

Homemade marshmallows made with fresh strawberries make a lovely gift packaged in clear cellophane bags and tied with ribbon or ricrac trim. For an extra special touch, slip a sachet of luxury hot chocolate into the bag so your guests can enjoy an indulgent treat when they arrive home after the wedding.

Put the strawberries in a food processor and blend to a smooth purée. Pour into a large mixing bowl and stir in the lemon juice. Sprinkle over the powdered gelatin and leave to soak.

Put the sugar, syrup, and ¾ cup water in a saucepan and heat very gently, stirring occasionally, until the sugar has completely dissolved. Bring to a boil and heat to 275°F, then remove from the heat and leave to cool for a couple of minutes.

Using an electric hand whisk on high speed, whisk the strawberry mixture until well blended. Reduce the speed to medium, then gradually drizzle the syrup down the edge of the mixing bowl, whisking all the time. Whisk for about 10 minutes until the mixture is very thick and throwing out strands from the beaters.

Pour the mixture into the lined baking pan and lay the sheet of greased plastic wrap over the top. Leave to set in a cool place for at least 2 hours until the marshmallow feels firm and set.

Peel off the plastic wrap and lightly dust the top of the marshmallow with about 1 tablespoon cornstarch. Turn out onto a board and peel off the remaining plastic wrap. Dust with more cornstarch, then cut into ¾-inch cubes using a sharp, greased knife (the cubes will be very sticky, so handle with care). Alternatively, cut rounds from the marshmallow using a small cookie cutter (you will end up with fewer marshmallows). Sift the remaining cornstarch onto a large plate and roll each marshmallow to coat. Toss well to remove any excess cornstarch.

Store the marshmallows in an airtight container until required. These can be made up to a week in advance.

white chocolate cake pops

2 tablespoons heavy
cream
2 tablespoons butter
3½ oz. white chocolate,
broken into chunks
6 oz. plain yellow cake,
finely crumbled

To decorate
7 oz. white chocolate,
broken into chunks
pink heart sugar sprinkles

20 sucker sticks

makes 20

These cuter-than-cute cake pops will make your guests smile as they sit down to enjoy the wedding feast. With a fudgy center and crisp white chocolate coating they are delicious and easy to make. Decorating them can be a great activity for the bride and her hens—possibly using a glass of champagne or two to channel their creative flair!

Put the cream, butter, and 3½ oz. white chocolate in a heatproof bowl set over a pan of barely simmering water. Leave to stand until melted, then remove from the heat and stir in the cake crumbs. Chill in the fridge for about 1 hour, until firm.

Take heaping teaspoonfuls of the mixture and roll into balls roughly the size of a small walnut. Gently insert a sucker stick into each one, then leave to chill and set overnight.

To decorate, melt the 7 oz. white chocolate in a heatproof bowl set over a pan of barely simmering water. Remove from the heat and leave to cool. Dip the cake pops in the chocolate, turning to coat, then decorate with the heart sugar sprinkles. Leave to set, then chill. (Shot glasses make a good place to stand your pops while they set.)

Store the cake pops in an airtight container until required. These can be made up to a week in advance.

golden dark chocolate truffles

8 oz. semisweet
chocolate, broken
into chunks

1 cup heavy cream

3 tablespoons butter,
diced

edible gold leaf,
for decorating

a melon baller

*a baking sheet, lined with
non-stick baking paper*

a soft brush

petits fours cases

makes about 40

Rich, buttery truffles make wonderful petits fours for a wedding, but coating them in a thin layer of edible gold leaf makes them even more special. Edible gold leaf is available over the internet and from cake decorating shops. It is supplied in thin sheets, interleaved with tissue paper. Look for tiny gift boxes and nestle a truffle inside each one. You may want to make your truffles slightly larger depending on the size of your chosen box.

Put the chocolate in a food processor and blitz until finely chopped, then transfer to a mixing bowl.

In a small saucepan, gently heat the cream and butter together until almost boiling, then pour over the chocolate in the mixing bowl and stir until smooth. Cover and chill in the fridge for about 4 hours, until the mixture is firm.

Scoop up rounds of the mixture using a melon baller, then gently roll into balls and place on the prepared baking sheet.

Chill again for about 1 hour, then gently roll the top half of each truffle on a sheet of gold leaf and press to the surface using the brush. Place each truffle in a petit four case and store in an airtight container in the fridge until required. These can be made up to a week in advance.

bite-size brownie squares

4 tablespoons butter

4½ oz. semisweet chocolate, broken into chunks

⅔ cup sugar

2 eggs

½ cup all-purpose flour

an 8-inch square cake pan, lined with non-stick baking paper

makes 36

Everyone loves rich, chocolatey brownies, so stack up these bite-size ones and bind with a strip of baking paper, finishing with a ribbon and a small posy of silk flowers. If you like your brownies nutty, throw a handful of walnut pieces into the mix when you add the flour.

Preheat the oven to 350°F.

Put the butter and chocolate chunks in a heatproof bowl and heat gently over a pan of barely simmering water until melted. Remove from the heat and leave to cool for about 5 minutes. Stir in the sugar, then beat in the eggs. Sift over the flour and fold in.

Pour the mixture into the prepared cake pan and bake in the preheated oven for about 17 minutes, until firm to the touch and pale on top. Leave to cool in the pan.

Turn the brownie out onto a chopping board and use a sharp knife to slice the square into 6 strips, then slice into 6 strips in the opposite direction to make 36 cubes.

Store the brownies in an airtight container until required. These can be made up to 4 days in advance.

floral baby cake bites

1 stick butter

½ cup plus 1 tablespoon sugar

2 eggs

½ teaspoon vanilla extract

scant 1 cup self-rising flour

2 tablespoons raspberry jam

To decorate

4½ cups confectioners' sugar

1 tablespoon golden or light corn syrup

½ teaspoon vanilla extract

blue, yellow, and pink food coloring

ready-made sugar flowers

2 x 8-inch square cake pans, greased and lined with non-stick baking paper

petits fours cases

makes 49

These pretty bite-size cakes make wonderful petits fours and look lovely arranged in paper cases on elegant cake stands on the tables. Use ready-made sugar flower decorations, which look professional and make your life a lot simpler! Most cake decorating shops and online stockists have a beautiful selection to choose from.

Preheat the oven to 350°F.

In a large mixing bowl, beat together the butter and sugar until pale and creamy. Beat in the eggs one at a time, then stir in the vanilla extract. Sift the flour over the mixture, then fold everything together.

Divide the mixture between the prepared cake pans and bake for about 13 minutes, until risen and the top springs back when gently pressed with a fingertip. Turn out onto a wire rack to cool.

When cooled, spread a thin layer of jam over one cake and place the second cake on top, patting down. Using a sharp knife, gently slice the cake into 7 strips, then slice into 7 strips in the opposite direction to make 49 cubes. Arrange the cubes on a wire rack, spacing well apart.

Put the confectioners' sugar, syrup, vanilla extract, and 4½ tablespoons water in a bowl and stir to combine. Divide the mixture between three heatproof bowls and tint each a different color. Place one bowl over a pan of barely simmering water, stirring, for 3 minutes. If the frosting remains very thick, add a drop of water at a time until you achieve a pouring consistency. Working quickly, spoon the frosting over one-third of the cakes and top each with a sugar flower whilst still sticky. (If the frosting becomes hard, return to the heat briefly until thinned.) Repeat with the remaining frosting and cake cubes, returning each to the wire rack to set. When the frosting is dry, place each cake in a petit four case.

Store the cake bites in an airtight container until required. The cake can be made a few days in advance, but it is best to leave the decorating until the day before the wedding.

cupcake place names

1 stick butter, at room temperature

½ cup plus 1 tablespoon sugar

2 eggs

scant 1 cup self-rising flour

To decorate

1 lb. ready-to-roll fondant icing

pistachio green food coloring (or a coloring of your choice)

confectioners' sugar, for dusting

2 tablespoons apricot jam, strained

a 12-hole cupcake pan, lined with paper or metallic cases

a round cookie cutter the same size as your cupcake cases

a 2-inch heart cookie cutter

12 toothpicks topped with name tags

makes 12

Save yourself a little time and energy by making pretty cupcakes that can be used as an edible favor and place card in one! Choose any color you like for the frosting—either tying in with the color scheme of the wedding for a sophisticated feel, or in vibrant pastels for a fun, playful look. Intricate, laser-cut cupcake wrappers lend a beautiful finish.

Preheat the oven to 350°F.

In a large mixing bowl, beat together the butter and sugar until pale and creamy, then beat in the eggs one at a time. Sift the flour over the mixture, then fold everything together until well incorporated.

Spoon the cake mixture into the cake cases and bake for about 18 minutes until risen and golden and the sponge bounces back when gently pressed with a fingertip. Carefully transfer the cakes to a wire rack and set aside to cool completely.

To decorate, slice the tops off any cakes that have domed up above the cupcake case. Tint 12 oz. of the fondant icing with the food coloring. Lightly dust a work surface with confectioners' sugar and roll out the fondant to a thickness of ⅛ inch. Stamp out 12 circles with the round cookie cutter. Using a pastry brush, brush the tops of the cakes with jam and gently press an icing circle onto the top of each cake.

Roll out the remaining (white) icing to about ¼ inch thick, then stamp out 12 hearts with the cookie cutter. Dampen the bottom of each heart with a little water and stick one on the top of each cake, finishing with a toothpick name tag.

Store the cupcakes in an airtight container until required. The cupcakes can be made a few days in advance, but it is best to leave the decorating until the day before the wedding.

french macarons

2 egg whites
pink food coloring
1 cup confectioners'
sugar
4 oz. (about ½ cup)
ground almonds
blackcurrant or
strawberry jam, to serve

*a piping bag fitted with a
large round tip*
*2 baking sheets, lined with
non-stick baking paper*

makes about 16 pairs

Pairs of pretty pastel-colored macarons make lovely favors, packaged
in little boxes. This recipe is for a single color but you can easily make
several batches in different colors. Pale green macarons look great
sandwiched with chocolate spread while yellow macarons are great
with a lemon curd filling.

Preheat the oven to 350°F.

Whisk the egg whites in a spotlessly clean, grease-free mixing bowl until they form stiff
peaks. Add a few drops of food coloring and whisk again briefly until just combined.

In a separate mixing bowl, combine the confectioners' sugar and almonds, then sift
over the egg whites and gently fold together. Spoon the mixture into the piping bag
and pipe ¾-inch rounds onto the prepared baking sheets, spacing well apart.

Bake the macarons in the preheated oven for 10 minutes. Remove from the oven and
leave to cool on the baking sheets for a few minutes before transferring to a wire rack
to cool completely.

To assemble, spread a thin layer of jam on half of the macarons and sandwich with
the remaining macarons. Store the macarons in an airtight container until required.
The macarons can be made up to 3 days in advance, but it is best to leave
sandwiching them together until the day before the wedding.

love heart tarts

1¾ oz. (about ¼ cup) ground almonds

1⅔ cups all-purpose flour, plus extra for dusting

2 tablespoons sugar

6½ tablespoons butter, chilled and diced

about 8 tablespoons raspberry jam

a round cookie cutter slightly larger than the pan holes

2 x 12-hole tart pans, greased

a 1½-inch heart cookie cutter

a 1-inch heart cookie cutter

makes 24

These sweet little almond and raspberry tarts look divine placed inside a gift box on a bed of crumpled tissue paper. Place one tart inside a square box, or a pair of hearts in a rectangular box, which look even more pretty if you vary the heart decoration on each.

Put the almonds, flour, and sugar in a food processor and pulse to combine. Add the butter and process until the mixture resembles fine breadcrumbs. Still processing, gradually add 3–4 tablespoons water, until the mixture comes together into a dough. Wrap the dough in plastic wrap and chill for at least 30 minutes.

Preheat the oven to 375°F.

Roll out the pastry on a lightly floured surface to about ⅛ inch thick. Stamp out 24 circles with the round cookie cutter, rerolling the pastry as necessary. Press the pastry rounds into the hollows of the prepared tart pans and prick the bases. Spoon a teaspoonful of jam into each tart.

Use the remaining pastry to cut out hearts using the 1½-inch cookie cutter. With the 1-inch cutter, cut hearts out of the centre of the larger hearts. Decorate some of the tarts with the small hearts and others with the large heart outlines. Bake in the preheated oven for about 12 minutes, until the pastry is golden. Transfer to a wire rack to cool completely.

Store the tarts in an airtight container until required. These can be made up to 2 days in advance.

cherry biscotti

Crisp, citrusy biscotti studded with dried cherries and almonds make a lovely coffee-time treat at the wedding, or can be easily transported home. They look beautiful bound together with a wide strip of decorative paper or ribbon.

2 eggs
grated zest of ½ orange
⅔ cup all-purpose flour
⅔ cup self-rising flour
½ cup fine cornmeal
scant ½ cup sugar
½ cup dried cherries
½ cup blanched almonds

a baking sheet, greased

makes about 20

Preheat the oven to 325°F.

Beat together the eggs and orange zest and set aside.

Combine the flours, cornmeal, and sugar and sift together into a large mixing bowl. Make a well in the centre and pour in the egg mixture. Add the cherries and almonds and stir together to combine, then knead gently to make a soft, sticky dough.

Shape the dough into a flat log about 8 inches long, 3 inches wide, and 1 inch high and place on the prepared baking sheet. Bake in the preheated oven for about 30 minutes until golden.

Remove the log from the oven (leaving the oven on) and allow to cool on the baking sheet for about 5 minutes. Transfer to a chopping board and use a serrated knife to gently slice the log into ⅜-thick slices.

Arrange the biscotti slices in a single layer on the baking sheet and bake for a further 15–20 minutes until crisp and golden. Transfer to a wire rack to cool.

Store the biscotti in an airtight container until required. These can be made up to 4 days in advance.

mini cupcakes

1 stick butter, at room temperature

½ cup plus 1 tablespoon sugar

grated zest of 1 lemon

2 eggs

scant 1 cup self-rising flour

To decorate

1½ sticks unsalted butter, at room temperature

3⅓ cups confectioners' sugar, sifted

3 tablespoons freshly squeezed lemon juice

food coloring in your choice of colors

sugar sprinkles

silver dragées

a 24-hole mini muffin pan, lined with paper cases

a piping bag fitted with a large star tip

makes 24

Baby cupcakes with a swirl of pretty pastel frosting and packaged in decorative boxes make a lovely gift for your guests, either to eat at the wedding or to take home and enjoy later. Look online for boxes to package your cakes in. To accommodate a pair of cupcakes you will need a box measuring approximately 4 inches x 2 inches x 3 inches high.

Preheat the oven to 350°F.

In a large mixing bowl, beat together the butter and sugar until pale and creamy. Beat in the lemon zest and then the eggs, one at a time. Sift the flour over the mixture, then fold everything together.

Spoon the cake mixture into the paper cases and bake in the preheated oven for about 15 minutes, until risen and golden and the sponge bounces back when gently pressed with a fingertip. Transfer the cakes to a wire rack and set aside to cool.

To decorate, beat together the butter, confectioners' sugar, and lemon juice with an electric hand whisk until smooth and creamy. Tint with the food coloring of your choice (or divide into two batches and tint two different colors) and briefly beat again to achieve an even color. Spoon the frosting into the piping bag and pipe a swirl on top of each of the cupcakes. (Repeat with the second batch of frosting, if using two colors.) Scatter with sugar sprinkles and finish with a silver dragée.

Store the cupcakes in an airtight container until required. The cupcakes can be made a few days in advance, but it is best to leave the decorating until the day before the wedding.

jewelled florentines

Sweet, melt-in-the-mouth florentines are the classic petit four and have a natural place in the list of edible wedding favors. These ones are coated in a thin layer of white chocolate, but they are delicious made with dark or milk chocolate, too. Arrange them on a decorative plate on the table or package up little stacks of florentines in delicate netting tied with ribbon.

3 tablespoons unsalted butter

¼ cup sugar

3 tablespoons heavy cream

2 tablespoons slivered almonds

¼ cup chopped pistachio nuts

2 tablespoons chopped walnuts

scant ½ cup mixed candied fruits, such as apricots, cherries, citrus peel, and angelica

2 tablespoons all-purpose flour

3½ oz. white chocolate, broken into chunks, to decorate

2 baking sheets, lined with non-stick baking paper and greased

makes 24

Preheat the oven to 350°F.

Put the butter, sugar, and cream in a large saucepan and heat very gently until the butter has melted. Bring to a boil, then remove from the heat and stir in the nuts, candied fruits, and flour.

Drop teaspoonfuls of the mixture onto the prepared baking sheets, spacing well apart. Bake in the preheated oven for about 10 minutes until golden. Remove from the oven and, while still warm, tidy the edges of each florentine by using a knife to press around the edge of each one to make neat rounds, then leave to cool for about 10 minutes. Carefully peel off the baking paper then transfer to a wire rack to cool completely.

Melt the chocolate in a heatproof bowl set over a pan of barely simmering water. Use a palette knife to spread the base of each florentine with a thin layer of melted chocolate. Leave to firm up slightly, then make a wavy pattern in the chocolate using the tines of a fork before leaving to set completely.

Store the florentines in an airtight container until required. These can be made up to 3 days in advance.

meringue kisses

2 egg whites
½ cup plus 1 tablespoon
superfine sugar

*a piping bag fitted with
a large round tip*
*2 baking sheets, lined with
non-stick baking paper*

makes about 50

There's something utterly irresistible about fluffy white meringues.
They look lovely tucked into boxes and tied with ribbon, or equally good
piled up on cake stands and scattered with pale pink rose petals. If you're
feeling more adventurous, you could even string them into garlands with
dried rosebuds or petals to decorate the tables or venue. If you're arranging
your meringues as a centerpiece or table decoration, serve with a little
dish of whipped cream and fresh strawberries, too, for guests to dunk.

Preheat the oven to 225°F.

In a spotlessly clean, grease-free bowl, whisk the egg whites with an electric hand
whisk until they stand in stiff peaks. Gradually add the sugar, a spoonful at a time,
whisking thoroughly between each addition until the mixture is thick and glossy.

Spoon the meringue into the piping bag and pipe swirls onto the prepared baking
sheets. Bake in the preheated oven for 1 hour until crisp and dry. Remove from the
oven and leave to cool.

Store the meringue kisses in an airtight container until required. These can be made
up to 4 days in advance.

celebration cookies

blossom cookies

These cookies have a lovely glossy, smooth frosting but despite their professional appearance they are deceptively simple to make. Choose any color of flower you like to match your wedding theme. Pretty pastels look good against the green stems.

6 tablespoons butter, at room temperature

½ cup sugar

1 egg yolk

1⅔ cups all-purpose flour

2 large egg whites

1 lb. confectioners' sugar, sifted

leaf green food coloring

lemon juice, for drizzling

ready-made sugar flowers or 7 oz. pink ready-to-roll fondant icing*

a 3-inch square cookie cutter (optional)

2 baking sheets, greased

2 piping bags fitted with small round tips

a blossom plunger cutter (optional)

makes 10

In a large mixing bowl, cream together the butter and sugar, then beat in the egg yolk. Sift the flour over the mixture and stir well to combine. Press the dough into a ball, wrap in plastic wrap, and chill for about 1 hour.

Preheat the oven to 350°F. Roll out the dough on a lightly floured surface to about ¼ inch thick and cut into 3-inch squares using a knife or cookie cutter. Place on the prepared baking sheets and bake for about 14 minutes until just coloring at the edges. Transfer to a wire rack to cool.

Beat the egg whites and confectioners' sugar together to make a thick frosting suitable for piping. Spoon one-quarter of the mixture into a separate bowl and tint green with the food coloring, then press a layer of plastic wrap over the surface to keep it fresh. Spoon about one-third of the white frosting into a piping bag and pipe a border around the cookies about ¼ inch from the edge. Add a little lemon juice to the remaining frosting in the bowl and stir to make a good drizzling consistency. Drizzle the thinner frosting inside the boundary lines to fill, then set aside to firm.

Spoon the reserved green frosting into the second piping bag and pipe delicate stems across the cookies. Using a small blob of frosting on the back of each flower, attach the sugar flowers to the stems and leave to set. When set, store the cookies in an airtight container until required. The cookies can be made up to 4 days in advance, but it is best to leave the decorating until only 1 or 2 days before the wedding.

*You can buy ready-made sugar flowers from cake-decorating shops, but they are very easy to make yourself using ready-to-roll fondant icing. Break off a chunk of icing and roll it out on a surface lightly dusted with confectioners' sugar. Cut out blossoms using a small blossom cutter. Using a palette knife, gently lift the flowers onto a curved flower former. Leave to dry completely before using to decorate your cookies. You can make the flowers several weeks in advance and store in an airtight container until required.

ribboned sugar cookies

These simple buttery cookies look pretty mixed and matched. Choose the color of the ribbon to match the color scheme of your wedding.

1 stick butter, at room temperature
¼ cup sugar, plus extra for sprinkling
1 egg yolk
1⅓ cups all-purpose flour
2 tablespoons milk, to glaze

To decorate
7 oz. ready-to-roll fondant icing

2 tablespoons apricot jam, strained
edible gold lustre

a 3-inch heart cookie cutter
2 baking sheets, greased
a drinking straw
a soft-bristled brush
14 lengths of organza ribbon

makes 14

In a large mixing bowl, cream together the butter and sugar, then beat in the egg yolk. Sift the flour over the mixture and stir well to combine. Tip the mixture out onto a lightly floured surface and knead gently to make a soft dough. Wrap in plastic wrap and chill for 30 minutes.

Preheat the oven to 350°F. Roll out the dough on a lightly floured surface to about ¼ inch thick. Stamp out hearts using the cutter and arrange on the prepared baking sheets. If making simple sugar-sprinkled cookies, use a pastry brush to lightly glaze the top of each cookie with milk and then sprinkle them generously with sugar, otherwise, leave them bare. Make a hole at the top of each cookie with the straw, then bake the cookies in the preheated oven for about 10 minutes or until pale golden. Leave to cool on the baking sheets for a few minutes, then transfer to a wire rack to cool completely.

For the iced cookies, roll out the fondant icing to ¹⁄₁₆ inch thick on a sheet of baking paper. Brush a thin layer of apricot jam over the cookies. With the cutter, stamp out hearts from the icing and use to top each of the cookies. Using the straw, make a hole in the icing above the original cookie hole. Using a soft-bristled brush, dust the cookies with gold lustre and leave to dry. You can achieve different effects by brushing on varying amounts of the lustre, or you could even leave some plain white.

Store the cookies in an airtight container until required. These can be made up to 3 days in advance. Thread each cookie with organza ribbon and tie in a bow.

confetti cookies

These cute cookies look adorable scattered over the tables. Frost them in your wedding colors or decorate them in pastel colors just like old-fashioned paper confetti. Look out for sets of mini cookie cutters in classic confetti shapes such as hearts, blossom, horseshoes, and clover.

1 cup plus 2 tablespoons all-purpose flour
6 tablespoons butter, chilled and diced
scant ½ cup sugar
1 egg yolk

To decorate
1⅔ cups confectioners' sugar

2 tablespoons lemon juice
food coloring (pastel lilacs, blues, greens, pinks, and yellows all work well)

mini heart, horseshoe, and flower cookie cutters (about 1 inch across)
2 baking sheets, greased

makes about 80

Put the flour and butter in a food processor and blitz until the mixture resembles fine breadcrumbs. Add the sugar and egg yolk and blitz until the mixture starts to come together. Turn out onto a lightly floured surface and knead until it forms a dough. Press into a ball, wrap in plastic wrap, and chill for at least 30 minutes.

Preheat the oven to 350°F. Roll out the dough on a lightly floured surface to about ¼ inch thick, then stamp out shapes using the cutters. Arrange on the baking sheets, then bake in the preheated oven for about 10 minutes until pale golden. Transfer to a wire rack to cool.

To decorate, sift the confectioners' sugar into a bowl, then stir in the lemon juice to make a smooth, thick frosting, adding a little more water if necessary. Divide into smaller bowls (according to how many colors you want to decorate your confetti) and tint each bowl of frosting a different color. Dip each cookie face down into a bowl of frosting, allow the excess to drizzle off, then turn right-side up and leave to dry on the wire rack.

Store the cookies in an airtight container until required. The cookies can be made up to 4 days in advance, but it is best to leave the decorating until only 1 or 2 days before the wedding.

gingerbread loveheart napkin ties

1 stick butter, at room temperature

½ cup packed soft light brown sugar

1 egg

⅓ cup golden or light corn syrup

3 cups plus 2 tablespoons all-purpose flour

1 teaspoon ground ginger

2½ oz. white chocolate, to decorate

a 2½-inch heart cookie cutter

a drinking straw

2 baking sheets, greased

a piping bag fitted with a small round tip

16 x 28-inch lengths ¼-inch wide satin ribbon

makes about 40

Why bother with napkin rings when you can use these cute and delicious gingerbread cookies instead? They look gorgeous and bring a fun twist to any wedding table. Decorate them simply or, if you are feeling creative, ice names on them and use them as a napkin ring, favor, and place setting in one. Choose ribbon colors to complement the table flowers.

In a large mixing bowl, beat together the butter and sugar until pale and creamy, then beat in the egg followed by the syrup. Sift the flour and ginger over the mixture and fold in. Turn out on to a lightly floured surface and knead gently to make a soft dough, then press into a ball, wrap in plastic wrap, and chill for 30 minutes.

Preheat the oven to 350°F.

Roll out the dough on a lightly floured surface to about ¼ inch thick. Cut out hearts using the cookie cutter and make a hole for the ribbon at the top of each heart using the drinking straw.

Arrange the cookies on the baking sheets and bake in the preheated oven for about 12 minutes until starting to color around the edges. Leave to cool for about 3 minutes on the baking sheet, then transfer to a wire rack to cool completely.

To decorate, break the white chocolate into a heatproof bowl set over a pan of barely simmering water. Stir until melted, then remove from the heat and leave to cool a little. Spoon the chocolate into the piping bag and pipe decorations, such as lines and dots or guests' names, on the cookies. Leave in a cool place to set.

Store the cookies in an airtight container until required. The cookies can be made up to 4 days in advance, but it is best to leave the decorating until only 1 or 2 days before the wedding.

To make the napkin ties, wrap the ribbon around the napkin, tying the cookies in place and secure with a knot, leaving the ends of the ribbon loose.

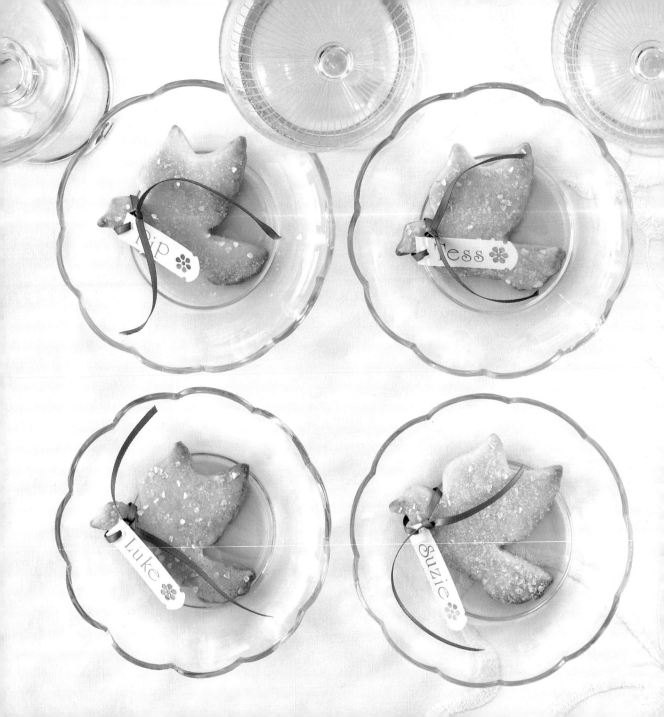

sparkling lovebird cookies

These simple sparkling sugar cookies look gorgeous nestled on your guests' folded napkins. They look good on both white or colored linen. You could also try sprinkling on a little silver or transparent edible sparkle, too.

1 stick butter, at room temperature

¼ cup sugar

1 egg

1⅔ cups all-purpose flour

1 tablespoon ground almonds

To decorate

⅓ cup confectioners' sugar

2 teaspoons lemon juice

granulated or sanding sugar, for sprinkling

edible glitter or sprinkles (optional)

a 3-inch dove cookie cutter

2 baking sheets, greased

makes about 24

In a large mixing bowl, beat together the butter and sugar until pale and creamy. Beat in the egg, then sift the flour and almonds over the mixture and fold in. Knead gently to make a soft dough, then press into a ball, wrap in plastic wrap, and chill for about 1 hour.

Preheat the oven to 350°F.

Roll out the dough on a lightly floured surface to about ⅛ inch thick and stamp out doves using the cookie cutter. Place the doves on the prepared baking sheets and bake in the preheated oven for about 10 minutes until the cookies are pale golden brown. Leave to cool for a couple of minutes on the baking sheets, then transfer the cookies to a wire rack to cool completely.

To decorate, mix together the confectioners' sugar and lemon juice until smooth. Brush a thin layer of the mixture over a cookie with a pastry brush and sprinkle generously with sugar. Repeat with the remaining cookies. When dry, shake off the excess sugar and sprinkle over a small amount of edible glitter or some sprinkles, if using.

Store the cookies in an airtight container until required. These can be made up to 4 days in advance.

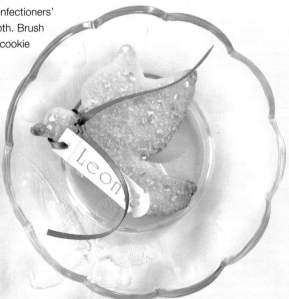

double chocolate name cookies

10 tablespoons butter,
at room temperature

¾ cup sugar

2 egg yolks

1¾ oz. semisweet
chocolate, melted

2⅓ cups all-purpose flour

2½ oz. white chocolate,
to decorate

*a 3-inch round, serrated
cookie cutter*

2 baking sheets, greased

*a piping bag fitted with
a small round tip*

makes 10

Getting your seating plan just right can be a stressful job, so inject some fun into it with these quirky name-card cookies. Go for the simple chocolate on chocolate approach or decorate with further embellishments such as gold or silver dragées. Tuck each cookie into a small envelope decorated with bows, flowers, or butterflies for a lovely decorative finish, as well as an easy way for your guests to take them home to enjoy.

Preheat the oven to 350°F.

In a large mixing bowl, beat together the butter and sugar until pale and creamy. Beat in the egg yolks, followed by the melted semisweet chocolate. Sift the flour over the mixture and fold in. Turn out onto a lightly floured surface and knead gently to make a soft dough, then press into a ball, wrap in plastic wrap, and chill for about 30 minutes.

Roll out the dough between two sheets of baking paper to about ⅛ inch thick. Cut out rounds with the cutter and arrange on the prepared baking sheets. Bake in the preheated oven for 10–12 minutes. Leave the cookies to cool on the sheets for a few minutes, then, using a spatula, transfer the cookies to a wire rack to cool completely.

To decorate, break the white chocolate into a heatproof bowl set over a pan of barely simmering water. Stir until melted, then remove from the heat and leave to cool a little. Spoon the chocolate into the piping bag and pipe names in the center of the cookies, then decorate around the names with lines, squiggles, dots, and hearts. Leave in a cool place to set.

Store the cookies in an airtight container until required. The cookies can be made up to 4 days in advance, but it is best to leave the decorating until only 1 or 2 days before the wedding.

strawberry wedding preserve

Spread the love with beautifully presented jars of fruit conserve for your guests to take away. You can buy matching miniature jars, or create a more personal look using a mixture of different small jars, such as those used for spices, condiments, pastes, and baby food. Finish the jars with pretty fabric or luxurious lace tied on with ribbon or colored string and hand-written tags. These are great favors if you are worried about time as they can be made weeks or even a couple of months in advance.

3 lbs. strawberries, hulled
6¼ cups sugar
freshly squeezed juice of 2 lemons

10 small sterilized jars (see page 4)
10 fabric circles with a design of your choosing
string or ribbon

makes about 10 small jars

Quarter the strawberries and put them in a large, non-metallic bowl. Sprinkle over the sugar and lemon juice, then cover with plastic wrap and leave to stand overnight.

Tip the fruit mixture into a preserving pan and heat gently, stirring until the sugar has completely dissolved. Boil for 10–15 minutes to 220°F, skimming off any scum that rises to the surface. Stir, then carefully pour the preserve into the sterilized jars using a funnel. Seal immediately and leave to cool.

Decorate your jars with rounds of fabric tied around the neck with a piece of string or ribbon. You could also add a hand-written gift tag for an extra-personal touch.

hazelnut and almond praline clusters

½ cup plus 1 tablespoon sugar

½ cup hazelnuts

⅔ cup slivered or split blanched almonds

a large baking sheet, greased

makes about 8 packages

These golden, nutty caramel bites taste divine and look gorgeous wrapped up in simple cellophane packages tied simply with ribbon or decorated with other ornaments, such as these cute buttons. Break into small pieces and apportion several per package, or break off larger chunks and wrap individually.

Put the sugar in a large, heavy-based pan and heat gently over a low–medium heat, without stirring, until the sugar starts to melt. At this point, stir to mix thoroughly and continue to heat until clear and pale golden.

Add the hazelnuts and almonds to the pan, stir, and cook for about 1 minute. Tip the caramel-coated nuts out onto the prepared baking sheet, spreading out gently. Leave to cool for about 20 minutes before breaking into pieces.

If packaging immediately, make sure the nuts are completely cool first. Otherwise, store the praline clusters in an airtight container until required. These can be made up to a week in advance.

golden caramel popcorn

Sweet, sugary popcorn coated in golden drizzles of caramel look gorgeous piled into cones made from decorative paper. If the idea of making your own cones is too much, try piling the popcorn up into decorative paper cups or brightly colored candy-striped bags.

1 tablespoon sunflower oil
½ cup popcorn kernels
1 cup plus 2 tablespoons sugar
⅓ cup golden or light corn syrup

2 baking sheets, greased

makes about 12 bags

First prepare the popcorn. Heat the oil in a large, heavy-based, lidded saucepan, with a couple of kernels in the pan. Once you hear those pop, add the rest of the popcorn kernels to the pan and cover with a lid. Shake the pan now and again as the kernels start to pop and continue heating until the popping stops. Remove from the heat and spread the popcorn out on the prepared baking sheets.

To make the caramel, put the sugar, syrup, and a scant ½ cup water in a saucepan and heat very gently, stirring occasionally, until the sugar has dissolved. Bring to a boil and, without stirring, heat to 275°F. (If you don't have a sugar thermometer, drop a little of the syrup into a glass of chilled water. When cool, you should be able to pull it into firm, pliable threads.) Remove from the heat and carefully drizzle the syrup over the popcorn.

Leave to cool completely, then lift the popcorn off the baking sheets with a metal spatula and break up any large chunks that have stuck together.

Store the popcorn in an airtight container until required. These can be made up to 4 days in advance.

candy apples

10 well-flavored apples,
such as braeburn
or pink lady

2¼ cups raw cane sugar

3 tablespoons butter

4 tablespoons golden
or light corn syrup

*10 wooden candy apple
sticks or short, slim dowels*

*a baking sheet, lined with
non-stick baking paper*

makes 10

Lovely for a fall wedding, these sweet apples have a wonderfully nostalgic feel and look gorgeous wrapped in clear cellophane and tied with colored string and a decorative leaf. Tie on a gift tag from the bride and groom or simply pop an apple in the center of each place setting.

Wash the apples in warm, soapy water, then rinse well and pat dry. Push a candy apple stick or short length of dowel into each apple.

Put the sugar and ¾ cup water into a heavy-based saucepan and warm over a gentle heat, stirring occasionally, until the sugar has dissolved. Stir in the butter and syrup, then bring to a boil and continue to boil (without stirring) until the mixture reaches 275°F. (If you don't have a sugar thermometer, drop a little of the syrup into a glass of chilled water. When cool, you should be able to pull it into firm, pliable threads.) Remove the saucepan from the heat and quickly but carefully, dip each apple in the toffee, turning until well coated. Leave to set on the prepared baking sheet.

When completely set, store the apples in an airtight container until required. These can be made up to 2 days in advance.

elderflower cordial

Sharp, sweet and tongue-tinglingly fragrant, this pretty pale pink cordial makes the perfect gift for your guests to take away and enjoy with sparkling water. Depending on the time of year you plan to get married, bear in mind that this recipe freezes well, so you can always make the cordial when elderflowers are in season and freeze it until the wedding day. Choose flower heads with creamy white open petals that are not yet beginning to drop.

2 lbs. sugar
2.5 quarts boiling water
pink food coloring
1 package citric acid (available from pharmacists)
30 elderflower heads

2 thinly sliced lemons

small sterilized bottles (see page 4)

makes about 2 litres

Put the sugar in a large heatproof bowl and pour over the boiling water. Add a few drops of food coloring to make a delicate pink cordial and stir until the sugar has dissolved. Set aside to cool.

Stir the citric acid into the cooled mixture. Gently rinse the flower heads then add to the sugar syrup along with the lemons. Leave to stand for 24 hours, stirring occasionally.

Strain the mixture through a muslin and bottle in sterilized bottles.

index

conversion chart

Weights and measures have been rounded up or down slightly to make measuring easier.

Measuring butter:

A US stick of butter weighs 4 oz which is approximately 115 g or 8 tablespoons.

Volume equivalents:

American	Metric	Imperial
1 teaspoon	5 ml	
1 tablespoon	15 ml	
¼ cup	60 ml	2 fl oz
⅓ cup	75 ml	2½ fl oz
½ cup	125 ml	4 fl oz
⅔ cup	150 ml	5 fl oz (¼ pint)
¾ cup	175 ml	6 fl oz
1 cup	250 ml	8 fl oz

Weight equivalents:

Imperial	Metric
1 oz	30 g
2 oz	55 g
3 oz	85 g
3½ oz	100 g
4 oz	115 g
5 oz	140 g
6 oz	175 g
8 oz (½ lb)	225 g
9 oz	250 g
10 oz	280 g
11½ oz	325 g
12 oz	350 g
13 oz	375 g
14 oz	400 g
15 oz	425 g
16 oz (1 lb)	450 g

Measurements:

Inches	Cm
¼ inch	5 mm
½ inch	1 cm
¾ inch	1.5 cm
1 inch	2.5 cm
2 inches	5 cm
3 inches	7 cm
4 inches	10 cm
5 inches	12 cm
6 inches	15 cm
7 inches	18 cm
8 inches	20 cm
9 inches	23 cm
10 inches	25 cm
11 inches	28 cm
12 inches	30 cm

Oven temperatures:

150°C	300°F	Gas 2
170°C	325°F	Gas 3
180°C	350°F	Gas 4
190°C	375°F	Gas 5
200°C	400°F	Gas 6